Published by Out-Spoken Press,
Future Studio,
237 Hackney Road,
London, E2 8NA

A CIP record for this title is available from
the British Library.

First edition published 2019
ISBN: 978-1-9996792-3-1

Design & Art Direction
Ben Lee

Printed & Bound by:
Print Resource

Typeset in: Baskerville

Out-Spoken Press is supported using public
funding by the National Lottery through
Arts Council England.

Ways of Coping

Ollie O'Neill

Child, all that anger could curdle the ocean

let it.

Ways of Coping

Contents

Mistake

Even his mother curses
in the shape of him.

When the tea spills or the mug breaks,
she measures his name against his neck.

Birth

"A BPD female is the closest thing you'll ever come to a modern-day siren. They can truly be the girls of your dreams, but they will lead you into a nightmare if you let them."

The phoenix setting itself alight
because it can. The doctor says
mania & I hear the door slam
then swing back open again,
daring me to dart, to see whether
I can make it through or if I'll catch
my elbow in the hinge until a bruise.

The doctor says mania & I
unscrew the sex letting it spill
like syrup to see who sticks,
sifting flies from their sugar
where I sit licking fingers.

The doctor says mania & I
am not listening, the sun
coming through the window
in such a way it must be deliberate,
God's own hand brushing my forearm
with all the resident seasons.

I know it's more ashes
than it is reinventing.

The doctor says
Borderline Personality Disorder -
when I get home I Google those words
to learn what I already knew.

That I am a special breed:
        fuckable
                unlovable

which came first
the chicken or the trauma?

The doctor says
Borderline Personality Disorder &
I am only half human.

The doctor says
mania & I
am alight
again.

Split

"If the hysteric was a damaged one, the borderline woman is a dangerous one."
– *Mary Ann Jimenez*

The cure was once to suck the womb out
through a straw. Women cannot be trusted
with anything, especially their own anatomy.

When you say every man is a room
with the walls closing in, out comes
a stethoscope or a speculum

contrary to popular belief
both halves of a worm won't survive
once split.

They just want to ask you some questions:
Are your breasts sagging?
Have you ever flinched under a full moon?
Do you leave the house without make-up?
Do you recognise yourself?
Would you like the 'husband's stitch'?

When you hear the word
can you match the shade of the bruise
to the blue of your blouse?

Can you show us
the exit wound?

Frolics

If I didn't want the corners
of my mouth where my lips meet
to crack   like the earth in the deepest heat
I should have just kept them closed.

The smell of bread baking
the ripest blackberry still blessing
its bush, underwear left in the
cutlery drawer.

Hunger

"Borderline women are dangerous - in their wake they leave men who are broke, incarcerated, demonised, and sometimes dead. That's not a joke or hyperbole. It is a fact of life."

Between taking and taken
you crouch down inside yourself
and begin repenting.

What is more erotic than forgiveness
when to want is also to apologise.

I watched you swallow the whole sky
until it was a purple feeling
felt the ache in your stomach
touched your working skin
thinned my name until it was hymnal.

If I took your hand to a glistening cunt
then to a damp cheek could you understand
the difference?

There is a hunger we don't know
how to feed.

We've offered him a chapel
but his belly is too big to be a heaven.

I try to stay be delicate
breakable but each time I blink
I break my eyelids.

I dream of being almost.

Guilt is a man trying to please me
two horses drinking where a river was.

Ask me what I want and I'll tell you
to make it swift, a fist through a spider's web.

Detergent

"Up to 53.8% of patients with BPD also meet criteria for an eating disorder"

before the session starts, I put in a disclaimer
I am the biggest I've been

which lets them know I am not so stupid
as to think that I am still small
      small enough to not let anybody touch me
to peel my clothes off   a wet plaster
see a vein disappearing underneath.

I had my own superpower once   invisibility
      appetite

I was so small I forgot the taste of everything
but tendon

now I'm the biggest I've been
I'll devour light, chew on the glass

bring it to me
my mouth has always been
big enough for punishment.

Applause

I know womanhood
is just the thought of iron.

Occupying an excuse.

The world demanding we are beautiful
in surviving.

Forward

"My only problem with 'Borderline Personality Disorder' is that, to some extent, the 'condition' describes literally every female alive."

Bathtub. Teacup. Basin.
All small lakes to drown in.

The first time I practice time travel,
I rip exits from my daydream,

bursting a blood vessel
in my right eye.

I am a pioneer of impatience,
it's paid off.

When they ask what year I travelled to
I'll shrug saying all of them.

Those knowing women will nod.
What chance have we got now

immodesty is the size of a tongue bar,
thick as a tendril.

The lips and the lipo
the bronzer and the blusher

it's important to wear your good hat
when you usher death.

Disappear

"This moment is exactly as it should be, given what's happened before it."

The baby is crying out for another baptism / just can't get close enough to God / Jesus wept and well he might / we are all changed by what we bring to our lips / lover / liquor / a man's thumb so large it fills my whole mouth / I saw you in the off-licence / on the middle shelf practicing / I am unfurling against your death / like the wind let it batter me / so inevitable /

the first time I meet my psychiatrist she presents a scenario to the group / a young boy no more than six / is killed / hit by a car on an intersection / flung from his bike / she asks us all if we think the boy should have died / I say no / remember tiny coffins / how I have seen one so small / so precious / a ring box / an occasion / a diamond in reverse back to coal / but she says / this was a test / the answer / yes / some things just happen and we must accept them / no matter how distasteful / that day the boy rode his bike / the car was already on its way /

I am remembering my first drink / was it red wine at the altar / or Guinness in your womb / two of us bonding / my unborn / thick and numb / becoming / accepting the hard swell your body offers / protecting itself from itself / I know what it is to get dizzy on self-destruction / how often it tastes like self-preservation / how long will you last like this / have you ever thought of death properly / do you know which song you'll disappear to / have you considered how quickly your body will be set to flames / with all that spirit inside you.

Virtuoso

"9 out of 10 sluts suffer from a Cluster B Personality Disorder. If you can learn to recognise Cluster B traits, you can avoid them (suggested) or, if you're disciplined enough use them for sex."

That's
not what
your mouth
is for -
you are
supposed to
abstain. Hold
back from
all the
world has
to offer.
Listen. To
me. Did
you know
that some
women cut
their food
into smaller
pieces before
they allow
themselves to
have it
if they
know
men are
watching? No
serpent could
talk them
into taking
now. They
know they
should fuck
the way
they eat.
They have
practiced
denying
their desires
for
lifetimes.
Have
it down
to an
art form.

Ways of Coping

Omen

"Emptiness and boredom: what a complete understatement.
What I felt was complete desolation. Desolation, despair and boredom."

If they sliced your stomach with the same ease as gliding a new knife
across cotton bed sheets, same white, same opening, and all they
found was a bird mid-flight, thirteen olive stones, an airplane trying
to hide the sun would it matter? I am trying to create a sense of
urgency. I don't mean to alarm anybody but yesterday, after the x-ray,
they pulled the black violin right from the gut, and before I could
form an excuse they sent me on my way. It has always been like this. I can
count the omens I saw last week: three dead dogs outside the tube station
and everyone just ignoring them. A couple of pigeons pecking sick near the
newsagents, then the van. Its bonnet a wrinkled brow, the dull flashing
of sirens when no emergency is left to have, just the smell of again.

Prescription

"Risk taking: Engagement in dangerous, risky, and potentially self-damaging activities, unnecessarily and without regard to consequences; lack of concern for one's limitations and denial of the reality of personal danger."

Yesterday, I timed how long it took
to burn the marrow from the bone.
Bent my whole self out of sex,
ate my own weight in dry cereal.
As the nurse fits the IV, I tell her
I have ways of coping
when I'm haemorrhaging memory,
being denied the simple pleasure of forgetting:

I take too much Aripiprazole or not enough
Lamotrigine, strip with the blinds open, double check
my symptoms, re-diagnose myself just in case.
I run my body through an online translation service,
skipping therapy.

When I really need to, I shove each tooth
back into the gum. Throw a welcome home party.

Venus

"Patients do not form confidential and/or romantic/sexual relationships with each other."

You look round the crisis house with me as though we are ready to buy a home, a married couple about to begin the rest of our lives together - who will carry the baby?

The mirrors are made of plastic, the bed sheets impossible. Connect Four and biscuits in the living room. It's highly egotistical for anybody to assume I couldn't hurt myself here.

The nurse asks if you are my lover the way one might gently nudge a sleeping dog just to be sure it isn't dead. I look at the ceiling. It's easier than truth, we are both destined

to get what we want, it will kill us eventually, all that desire and demand, high femme and high fatality, hysteria and hyperbole.

It's because we're both ruled by Venus you tell me later. We continue to pick the ECG glue from my skin and eat red cupcakes with our hands. When I slice my knuckle on a set of keys

opening a warm cider, you shove my whole finger in your mouth as though the cure is to just consume completely, until the blood stops.

I want to write my sex into verse,
but it spills,

             won't rhyme, doesn't fit,

never finishes.

Misandry

He says women are a lot like fruit

        in that there is a small window of ripeness before

                      the rot sets in.

He picks residual pieces from between his fingers.
He who insists on haunting
everything he enters.

Rooms, conversations

               bodies.

Encore

"Patients with BPD have an 8% to 10% increased risk of completed suicide"

by the time you fall asleep with a blade in the bed
you have run out of dying to do

you imagine waking to find the blade under your top lip
a whole new row of front teeth when you speak

a way to keep reflecting or maybe waking
to find it flat against your thigh where it's thickest

begging for stillness the problem with all of this doing
is when it's done.

Afterword

I wrote these poems exploring the overlap in the Venn diagram between crazy and woman. I wrote these poems after being diagnosed with Borderline Personality Disorder and spending six months in intensive group therapy before being kicked out, just before it was decided the service would be cut.

75% of people diagnosed with Borderline Personality Disorder are women. An innumerable amount of these women have experienced sexual trauma.

These poems are an attempt to understand how we differentiate between being mentally unwell and learning to survive, trying to find the point at which the female experience ends and the pathologising begins. And an effort to navigate a diagnosis that is, at its core, rooted in misogyny.

The epigraphs for these poems have been taken from a number of sources including studies, journals and blog posts. During my research, I discovered the seemingly endless number of forums and websites created by men to discuss women with Borderline Personality Disorder - from which I have also lifted quotations.

Acknowledgements

An endless thank you to Joelle Taylor, without whom not only this pamphlet, but every poem I've written since meeting her would not have been possible.

Thank you to Anthony Anaxagorou and Out-Spoken Press for giving me the chance to write and publish this pamphlet.

Thank you to William, for his endless patience.

Thank you to Miranda, for speaking the same soul language as me.

Thank you to Tal, for always knowing my truth and dragging me through it.

Sources

p3
"The Borderline Personality Disorder (BPD) and why you should run like hell"
*https://www.reddit.com/r/TheRedPill/comments/2l7mbw/
the_borderline_personality_disorder_bpd_and_why/*

p4
Mary Ann Jimenez, *Gender and Psychiatry: Psychiatric Conceptions of Mental Disorders in Women*, 1960-1994, Affilia (1997 July; Vol.2(2):154-175)

p6
"An Ear For Men: Six Subtle Gateways to Borderline Hell"
https://www.youtube.com/watch?v=iihsbrwqZLU

p7
MC Zanarini, CA Reichman, FR Frankenburg, DB Reich, G Fitzmaurice,
The course of eating disorders in patients with borderline personality disorder: a 10-year follow-up study, Int J Eat Disord. (2010 Apr; 43(3):226-32) cited at https://www.
clearviewwomenscenter.com/blog/BPD-eating-disorders/

p9
"think BPD is a fake disorder when it comes to being scientifically as legit as bipolar or schizophrenia,"
http://www.goingyourownway.com/mgtow-lounge/bpd-fake-disorder-comes-scientifically-4623/

p10
Matthew McKay, Jeffrey C. Wood, Jeffrey Brantley, *The Dialectical Behavior Therapy Skills Workbook: Practical DBT Exercises for Learning Mindfulness, Interpersonal Effectiveness, Emotion Regulation & Distress Tolerance* (New Harbinger Publications, 2017)

p11
"Dealing with Women with a Personality Disorder (specifically Cluster B)"
http://www.simplepickup.com/forum/questions-advice/2941-dealing-women-personality-disorder-specifically-cluster-b.html

p12
Susanna Kaysen, Girl, Interrupted, (Turtle Bay Books,1993)

p14
Diagnostic criteria for Borderline Personality Disorder, the Diagnostic
and Statistical Manual of Mental Disorders (5th ed.; DSM–5; American
Psychiatric Association, 2013)

p15
Highgate Personality Disorder Unit's guidelines to participating in
Dialectical Behavioural Therapy skills training, 2017

p17
Winston Smith Don't Date Girls with Borderline Personality Disorder
*http://www.returnofkings.com/9482/dont-date-girls-with-borderline-personality-
disorder*

p18
Joel Paris, Personality Disorders Over Time
(Washington DC: American Psychiatric Press. 2003)

Other titles by Out-Spoken Press:

A Greek Verse for Ophelia & Other Poems
Giovanni Quessep

The Games
Harry Josephine Giles

Songs My Enemy Taught Me
Joelle Taylor

To Sweeten Bitter
Raymond Antrobus

Dogtooth
Fran Lock

How You Might Know Me
Sabrina Mahfouz

Heterogeneous
New & Selected Poems
Anthony Anaxagorou

Titanic
Bridget Minamore

Out-Spoken 2015
An Anthology of Poetry
Out-Spoken Press

A Silence You Can Carry
Hibaq Osman

Email:
press@outspokenldn.com